EXPLORE WINTER!

Maxine Anderson
illustrated by Alexis Frederick-Frost

nomad press

green press INITIATIVE

Nomad Press is committed to preserving ancient forests and natural resources. We elected to print this title on 30% post consumer recycled paper, processed chlorine free. As a result, for this printing, we have saved:

5 Trees (40' tall and 6-8" diameter)
1,731 Gallons of Wastewater
3 million BTU's of Total Energy
222 Pounds of Solid Waste
417 Pounds of Greenhouse Gases

Nomad Press made this paper choice because our printer, Thomson-Shore, Inc., is a member of Green Press Initiative, a nonprofit program dedicated to supporting authors, publishers, and suppliers in their efforts to reduce their use of fiber obtained from endangered forests.

For more information, visit www.greenpressinitiative.org

Environmental impact estimates were made using the Environmental Defense Paper Calculator. For more information visit: www.papercalculator.org.

Many thanks to Patricia Murray for her insightful comments and advice.

Contents

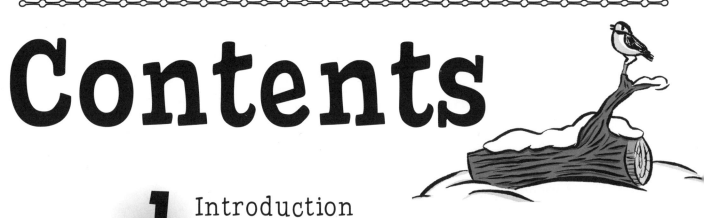

Other titles in Explore Your World! series

Praise for other books by Maxine Anderson

Great Civil War Projects You Can Build Yourself

"A fascinating gem of a book…"
—*The New York Times Book Review*

"Providing an intriguing look at Civil War history, this project mind teases the mind and invites the creative hand . . ." —*KLIATT Reviews*

"Includes little-known facts that will interest children unfamiliar with the conflict and Civil War buffs alike . . . A useful resource for any Civil War curriculum." —*School Library Journal*

"An engaging means for children to learn about the Civil War." —*Children's Literature*

"An interesting and creative book that should give pleasure as well as knowledge to many children."
—James McPherson, Pulitzer Prize–winning author of *Battle Cry of Freedom*

"A fascinating, interactive history of the Civil War along with daily life on the home front and on the battlefield." —*VOYA magazine*

Amazing Leonardo da Vinci Inventions You Can Build Yourself

"Anderson regales us with tales of Leonardo's brilliant, often mischievous nature, and the nearly unfathomable range of his inventions."
—*The New York Times Book Review*

"More than an activity book, this nifty volume explores Leonardo's life, times and endless imagination." —*Seattle Post-Intelligencer*

"Bring[s] an immediacy to da Vinci's life and work." —*Publishers Weekly*

"Creative, curiosity-provoking, informational, and just plain fun—kids will find it irresistible."
—*Home Education Magazine*

"This marvelous book will introduce you to some of Leonardo's most exciting ideas and innovations. Best of all, you get to build machines and explore the world much like Leonardo himself did."
—David Kaiser, Physicist and Historian of Science, Massachusetts Institute of Technology

Why Do We Have Winter, Anyway?

Brrr, it's cold outside! Days are shorter and nights are longer. The sun isn't very warm, even on the brightest days. And where did the flowers and insects go?

In some places **winter** can bring lots and lots of snow. In others, winter means chilly nights and cool days. But why do we have winter at all, and why does it happen at the same time every year?

This book is going to take a closer look at winter—the season between fall and spring. It is a time when it seems as if the natural world has gone to bed for a long nap. But as you read this book you will see that winter is a time for great explorations, both inside and outside.

You'll get to do lots of experiments and projects to learn more about winter.

You'll find out some interesting stuff. And you'll learn some silly jokes and amazing facts, too. So put on your warm, fuzzy slippers and get ready to learn about the season of winter!

Be a Scientist!

Most of the projects and activities in this book will have you ask questions and then try to come up with the answers: that's what scientists call the **scientific process**. It's the way scientists study the world around them. What's really interesting about the scientific process is that you can't just ask a question, answer it, and then be done. You have to prove every answer you give so other people can get the same answer using the same method you did. Here's how the scientific process works:

1. You ask a question or have an idea about something, called a **hypothesis**.

2. Then you come up with ways, or **experiments** to answer the question or prove your idea.

3. You do the experiment to see if you can prove your idea.

4. You change your idea based on the result of your experiment.

What Kind of Scientists Study the Seasons?

Lots of scientists study winter weather. A scientist who helps to predict the weather this week is called a **meteorologist**. If you want to know whether to wear a T-shirt and sandals or a parka and boots, you should ask a meteorologist. Another type of weather person is called a **climatologist**. A climatologist looks at weather that has already happened to find weather patterns that can predict future weather. If you want to know what the weather will look like next year or in 2015 or 2050 you would ask a climatologist.

What else do scientists do?

collect

Scientists **collect:** they gather things to observe them.

observe

Scientists **observe:** they notice what changes and what stays the same.

sort

Scientists **sort:** they organize the things they gather into different groups.

The word "winter" comes from an old German word that means "time of water." That makes sense, since snow and ice are made of water.

WOW!

Words2Know

winter: the season between fall and spring.

scientific process: the way scientists ask questions and do experiments to try to prove their ideas.

hypothesis: an unproven idea that tries to explain certain facts or observations.

experiment: testing an idea or hypothesis.

meteorologist: a scientist who studies weather patterns and makes weather predictions.

climatologist: a scientist who studies weather and climate from the past to predict weather and climate over a long period of time and a large area.

Make a Science Journal

One thing you'll do to find the answers to your questions is to look at things very carefully to see how they are changing. Then you'll write down the changes you notice. Many scientists use a science journal to keep track of what they see. You can, too. You can use any notebook for a science journal, or even just a few sheets of paper to write down what you see and do. You don't need anything fancy. But if you would like to make a special science journal, here's a fun way using construction paper, coffee filters, and cardboard. Since you will use scissors and a hole punch for this activity, make sure you have a grownup around to help.

1 Fold the pieces of white paper in half. Now you will have folded paper that measures 8½ by 7 inches.

2 Cut the pieces of cardboard to 7 by 9 inches. Put glue on one side of each of the cardboard pieces. It doesn't matter which side because you will cover it up.

3 Turn over each cardboard piece so the gluey side is down. Center it on the construction paper. Push down on the cardboard to make sure it sticks tight to the construction paper.

4 Make two diagonal cuts at each cardboard corner. You will cut away the corners of the construction paper. This will make it easy to fold over the extra construction paper onto the cardboard.

5 Put glue all the way around on the extra construction paper surrounding each piece of cardboard and fold it over onto the cardboard.

6 Now put glue on one side of the colored paper and glue it to the cardboard. Do this for each piece of cardboard. This will cover up the rest of the cardboard and make a nice inside lining to your cover. Your cover is ready to be decorated!

Supplies

10 pieces of legal-size white paper, 8½ by 14 inches

ruler

scissors

2 pieces of cardboard from a cracker box or cereal box

glue stick, paste, or white glue

2 pieces of construction paper, any color, 8½ by 10 inches

2 pieces of colored paper like old wrapping paper, cut to 6½ by 8 inches

2 or 3 coffee filters, the small, white, basket kind

hole punch

3 brads or 3 rubber bands

7 Take one coffee filter and fold it in half. Fold it in half again. Fold it in half two more times. It will look like an ice cream cone.

8 Now make small snips in the folds and edges of the coffee filter with the scissors to make patterns. Do NOT cut all the way across the filter. When you open up your coffee filter you'll have a snowflake. This is for the front cover of your journal. You can make a second snowflake for the back cover if you like. Glue the snowflakes to the covers of your journal.

9 Use the hole punch to punch three holes about an inch from the fold on the white paper. Punch one hole near the top, one near the bottom, and one in the middle. These will be your journal pages. The holes will go on the left of your journal.

10 Put the folded white paper inside the front and back covers of your journal. Mark on the inside of the covers where the holes in the paper are.

11 Punch matching holes in the cover so when you put the paper inside the covers you can see straight through the front cover, the journal pages, and the back cover.

12 If you are using brads to complete your journal, you can fit them in each hole and fasten them onto the back cover. If you are using rubber bands, put one end of the rubber band through each hole and pull it through the other end of the rubber band. That will hold it tight. You can also use yarn, string, ribbon, or even a cut-up shoelace!

Where Did the Day Go?

Chapter 1

What are some of the ways you know that fall is changing to winter? Well, you notice that the tree branches have lost their leaves and it gets cold outside.

In some places it gets very cold. Ice covers the ponds and lakes, and white snow blankets the ground.

Because the part of the earth having winter is tilted away from the sun, it doesn't get as much direct sunlight. This is why the sun sits lower in the sky and why it sets so early. Less direct sun also means colder air.

In cold air, rain turns to snow. Plants die. It is too cold for insects, and there are no fresh, green leaves for caterpillars or animals to eat. The birds that feed on insects need to find food in warmer places so they fly south.

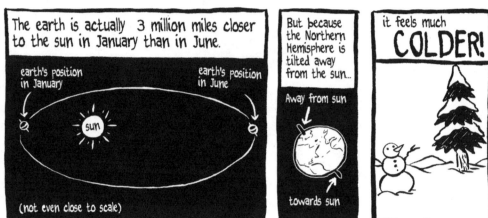

The earth is actually 3 million miles closer to the sun in January than in June.

earth's position in January

sun

earth's position in June

(not even close to scale)

But because the Northern Hemisphere is tilted away from the sun...

Away from sun

towards sun

it feels much COLDER!

Words 2 Know

cold-blooded: animals that need warm air or water to stay warm.

warm-blooded: animals that keep warm with their own body heat.

Northern Hemisphere: the half of the earth to the north of the equator.

equator: the imaginary line running around the middle of the earth that divides it in two halves, the Northern Hemisphere and the Southern Hemisphere.

Southern Hemisphere: the half of the earth to the south of the equator.

Cold temperatures make it hard for **cold-blooded** creatures like frogs, snakes, and turtles to move. Even **warm-blooded** animals like deer have a hard time finding enough food to stay healthy. So the natural world seems to shut down.

Why the Earth Has Seasons

You may live in a place where it is warm all year round. Or you may live in a place where it is cold in the winter, hot in the summer, and warm in the spring and fall. No matter where you live, your place on Planet Earth experiences seasons. The four seasons are spring, summer, fall, and winter, and the reason we earthlings have seasons has to do with the way the earth moves around the sun.

The earth travels slowly around the sun all the time. The sun is so big that it takes about 365 days for the earth to complete one full circle around the sun. We call that amount of time a year. While the earth moves around the sun, it spins like a top that is tilted to one side. The earth is always tilted in the same direction, and only part of the earth can be tilted toward the sun at one time. The part of the earth that is tilted toward the sun is having summer. That part is getting more direct sunlight than the part of the earth tilted away from the sun. And guess what? The part tilted away is having winter! In between summer and winter, when parts of the earth are moving from being tilted directly toward the sun to tilting directly away, you get spring and fall. That makes sense, right?

So the permanent tilt of the earth and its movement around the sun makes our year and our four seasons.

But winter in New York isn't winter in Australia. That's because New York is in the **Northern Hemisphere**, the half of the earth that is north of the **equator**. Australia is in the **Southern Hemisphere**, the half of the earth that is south of the equator. When the Northern Hemisphere is tilted away from the sun, having winter, the Southern Hemisphere is tilted toward the sun—having summer! How would you like to have summer in January?

WOW!

If you drove in a car at 65 miles an hour and never took a break, it would take you 163 years to travel the 93 million miles to the sun. If you hopped in a jet airliner that travels 500 mph it would take it 21 years to reach the sun!

Making Some

How does the tilt of the earth and the way it spins like a top while it circles the sun affect how much sunlight different parts get? It's much easier to understand when you see it in action!

1 Draw a line around the middle of your orange. That line will be the equator.

2 Put one thumbtack or sticker near the top of the orange and one thumbtack or sticker near the bottom. These will help you remember the Northern Hemisphere (top) and Southern Hemisphere (bottom) .

3 Hold your orange so your equator is parallel to the floor. Now push one toothpick into the top and another toothpick into the bottom of your orange. These are your North and South Poles. Push the toothpicks far enough into the orange so that you can hold the toothpicks and spin the orange around. One time around is a day.

4 Put the large bowl upside down on a small table for your sun. The sun is much, much bigger compared to the earth than this, of course. Mark a starting point on the bowl.

Sense of the Spin

5 Hold the orange by the toothpicks. Tilt the orange so the bottom toothpick, your South Pole, is slightly tilted toward the bowl, your sun. Slowly move the orange around the bowl. At the same time, spin the orange around itself while keeping it tilted.

As you first spin the orange around itself and also circle the bowl, you'll see that the bottom half of the orange (the Southern Hemisphere) faces the sun more directly. But what happens when you get about halfway around the bowl? The upper part of the orange, the Northern Hemisphere, faces the sun more directly. That's just what happens to the earth as it moves around the sun. Part of the year the Northern Hemisphere faces the sun more directly and has summer. That's when the Southern Hemisphere tilts away from the sun and has winter. Part of the year the Southern Hemisphere faces the sun more directly, and has summer while the Northern Hemisphere has winter. In between, neither hemisphere faces the sun more directly and they have spring or fall.

Supplies

an orange

black marker

2 thumbtacks or stickers of different colors

2 toothpicks

a large bowl

But Winter Doesn't Always Start on the First Day of Winter

Have you ever heard of the **winter solstice**? The official first day of winter is on December 21 and this is called the winter solstice. This is the day that the Northern Hemisphere tilts as far away from the sun as it will go. The winter solstice is the shortest day of the

WOW!

The heat from the sun takes more than 8 minutes to reach earth.

year. The **summer solstice**, on June 21, is the official first day of summer. This is the day that the Northern Hemisphere tilts toward the sun as much as it will go. The summer solstice is the longest day of the year.

But winter weather usually comes sooner than the first day of winter. Why? The Northern Hemisphere has been slowly tilting more and more away from the sun since the summer solstice. As the earth travels around the sun the sun's rays hit the Northern Hemisphere at more and more of an angle.

Late summer turns to fall. By the **fall equinox** on September 21, the official first day of fall, the weather is already cooler because the sun's rays hit a wider area and are less concentrated. The fall equinox is the day when there are 12 hours of daylight and 12 hours of darkness everywhere, no matter where you live.

Just for laughs

Q: How do you keep from getting cold feet in winter?

A: Don't go around BRRfooted!

Solstices and Equinoxes

winter solstice: December 21, the official first day of winter when the Northern Hemisphere tilts as far away from the sun as it will go. It's the shortest day of the year. In the Southern Hemisphere the winter solstice is June 21.

summer solstice: June 21, the official first day of summer, when the Northern Hemisphere tilts toward the sun as much as it will go. It's the longest day of the year. In the Southern Hemisphere the summer solstice is December 21.

fall equinox: September 21, the official first day of fall, when there is 12 hours of daylight and 12 hours of darkness everywhere, no matter where you live. In the Southern Hemisphere the fall equinox is March 21.

spring equinox: March 21, the official first day of spring, when there is 12 hours of daylight and 12 hours of darkness everywhere, no matter where you live. In the Southern Hemisphere the spring equinox is September 21.

It's when the Northern Hemisphere isn't tilted toward or away from the sun. The Southern Hemisphere isn't tilted toward or away either.

As the weeks pass you'll notice that the sun appears lower in the sky for shorter periods of time each day. By the time winter officially begins on December 21, the sun has reached its lowest point in the sky because the Northern Hemisphere is tilted the most away from the sun that it is going to get. Every day after this gets a little bit longer, as the Northern Hemisphere slowly starts tilting back toward the sun again.

shorter days

longer days

winter

spring

Latitude Decides Winter

Latitude is how far north or how far south you are from the equator. Think about the way the equator circles the earth, dividing it into two halves. The equator is 0 degrees latitude. Now look at the North Pole. That's 90 degrees latitude north (because you're north of the equator). In between the equator and the North Pole are all the numbers in between 0 degrees and 90 degrees. But it's too much work to draw all those lines!

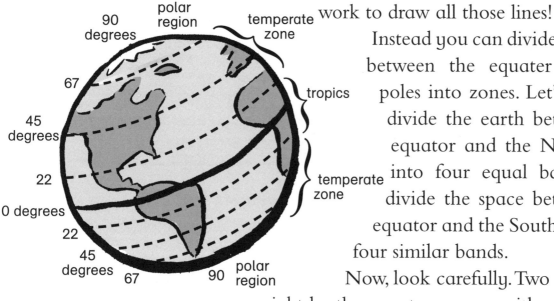

Instead you can divide the space between the equater and the poles into zones. Let's say you divide the earth between the equator and the North Pole into four equal bands. And divide the space between the equator and the South Pole into four similar bands.

Now, look carefully. Two bands are right by the equator, one on either side of it. This is called the tropics. It's hot there! And you've already learned that this is because the sun shines directly all year round. The two bands north of the tropics and the two bands south of the tropics are cooler. Another word for this is temperate. Scientists call this the temperate zone. The last two bands are farthest from the equator. One is right around the North Pole, the other right around the South Pole. These are the polar regions and it's really cold there!

How far you are from the equator—your latitude—determines your climate and what kind of winter you have. What kind of winter do you have?

The World is Divided into Biomes

A **biome** is a large area of the earth with a similar climate and similar plants and animals. Most of the land in the world is either near the equator or in the Northern Hemisphere, so there are more biomes there.

tundra: the coldest biome, around the North Pole. It's very cold in the long, dark winter. Moss and other low plants grow only in the few weeks of the summer. A lot of animals live in the tundra, like polar bears and caribou. The tundra gets as much rain as a desert!

taiga: this biome covers a lot of Canada, Europe, and Asia. It's the northern part of the temperate zone. Winter is cold with lots of snow. Evergreen trees like pine and spruce trees cover the taiga. Forest animals include moose and the bald eagle.

grassland: this biome is also in the temperate zone, between the forests and the desert. It is covered in tall grass that is good for grazing animals. Every continent except Antarctica has grassland. Closer to the equator, the climate of grasslands is hot all year. Farther from the equator winters are very cold and snowy and summers are very hot. There are not a lot of trees but there are lots of animals, like elephants, lions, and buffalo.

temperate forest: you can guess that this biome is also in the temperate zone. It has a hot summer, cool spring and fall, and cold winter. There is plenty of rain. Most of the trees lose their leaves in the fall and grow new ones in the spring. That way the snow can't pile up on the trees.

tropical rainforest: the seasons don't change much in this biome that is near the equator. It is hot and wet most of the time. It rains just about every day! This is the perfect climate for plants and animals and there are more here than anywhere else on the planet. Plants and animals include bananas, pineapples, oranges, lemons, palm trees, lizards, monkeys, and butterflies. Can you think of more?

desert: this biome gets very little rain. Deserts are usually to the north or south of tropical rainforests. While this is the hottest biome, deserts can get cold too. It's hard to imagine that plants and animals would live in the desert. But plenty do. Camels and cactus plants are famous desert animals and plants.

Why Is It Winter All the Time at the Earth's Poles?

Whether you live in the northern or southern part of the Northern Hemisphere, you know that eventually the seasons will change. When the winter solstice passes, the sun will shine a little longer each day.

Eventually, spring will come. The ground will thaw, and snow will melt away. But if you go to either the North Pole or the South Pole, you will discover that winter never really ends. Why? Because the poles don't ever get very much of the

The sun's outer surface is 10,000 degrees Fahrenheit.

sun's heat energy. The sun's rays never hit the polar regions directly, no matter where the earth is on its path around the sun. So the heat that reaches the earth at the poles is never as strong as it is near the equator. And since the poles are always covered in white snow and ice, a lot of the sun's energy that hits the ice and snow is reflected back into space.

sunlight

WOW!

The ice of Antarctica contains 70 percent of the earth's fresh water, but Antarctica itself is a desert. Less than 2 inches of water falls each year there. It is the largest and coldest desert in the world.

Winter Sun

Here's a way you can see how the sun's light and energy are not as strong on the part of the earth that is tilted away from the sun.

Go into a dark room. Turn on the flashlight and hold it so the beam is shining straight down onto the flat surface. You should be able to see a bright circle of light. Now hold the flashlight the same distance away, but turn the flashlight slightly so the beam of light is slightly tilted. Can you see how much more area the light has to cover when it is tilted? How about how much duller the light is when it is tilted and spread over a larger area? That is the same thing that happens to the sunlight in winter.

Supplies

dark room
flat surface
flashlight

Long Shadows

Don't winter days seem shorter than summer days? You're right—winter days ARE shorter than summer days. In winter, the sun never gets as high in the sky as it does during the summer because of the way the earth is tilted. In this experiment you can track how high the sun gets in the sky over a few weeks in the winter.

1 Open your folder, and with a pen and ruler draw a line down the crease on the folder. This will be called the crease line. Label one end of the crease line N to indicate the compass direction of north.

2 At the other end of the crease line about an inch from the edge, draw a second line parallel to the long edge and perpendicular to the line down the crease.

3 Place the center of the penny where the two lines cross. Trace around the penny so you have a drawing of a circle where the lines meet.

4 Take the folder outside and place it on a flat surface. Make sure you can either leave the folder there, or mark the location so you put the folder in the same spot each day. Also make sure that no large objects will block the sun from that spot during the day.

5 Use the compass to find north. Make sure the "N" on the folder is facing north.

6 Take the ball of clay and stick the toothpick through the center of the clay so it is sticking up like a flagpole.

Just for laughs

Q: How far can you see on a clear day?

A: 94 million miles . . . From here to the sun!

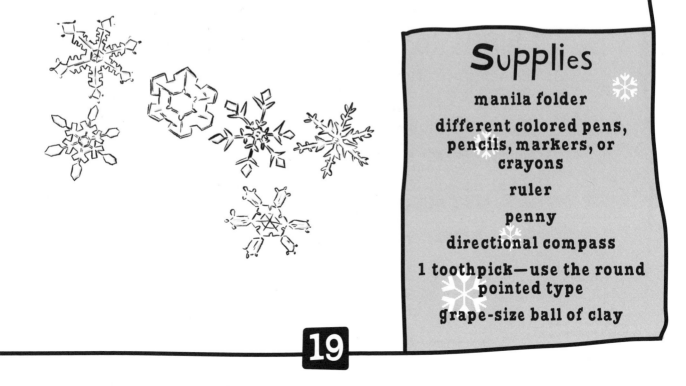

Supplies

manila folder

different colored pens, pencils, markers, or crayons

ruler

penny

directional compass

1 toothpick—use the round pointed type

grape-size ball of clay

7 Stick the clay on the circle you drew so the toothpick is standing straight up right in the middle of the circle. The toothpick will make a shadow in the sun.

8 Every day at noon, use a pen to mark the length of the toothpick's shadow on the folder. Label the date on the shadow.

9 Do this experiment every day for at least two weeks. Mark the shadow each day with a different color.

10 Measure and record the length of the shadow. Lift the clay and measure from the center of the circle where the lines cross to the end of the shadow.

Things to notice

❆ How many days did you measure the shadow?

❆ Did the shadow grow longer? If so, how much longer did the shadow grow every day?

❆ Did the shadow get shorter? If so, how much shorter?

❆ What do you think might have been different about the results of this experiment if you did it in the summer?

❆ What else did you notice about this experiment?

Coping with the Cold

Chapter 2

The tilt of the earth in winter means shorter days and longer nights in the Northern Hemisphere. It also means colder weather. The sun is lower in the sky so its light is less direct. Light and heat have to travel over more area. That means less sunlight.

Everything cools down: air, land, and oceans. Even the hottest places have shorter days and cooler temperatures in the winter. The hottest place in the United States is Death Valley, California.

In July, the temperature gets as high as 115 degrees **Fahrenheit** (46 degrees **Celsius**). That is really, really hot! But in December, the temperature in Death Valley is usually about 65 degrees Fahrenheit (18 degrees Celsius). That's almost 60 degrees colder than in summer—all because of the angle of the sun.

When it is colder outside, what do you do? Turn up the heat? Light a fire? Put on more clothes? What about creatures that live outside? It's hard to live through the winter outside. It's cold. It can be stormy. And it's hard to find food. What do animals and birds and insects do? They have different ways to cope with cold.

❄ They can **migrate** ❄ They can **hibernate** ❄ They can **adapt** ❄

Some Animals Migrate

To migrate means to travel to the same place at the same time each year. Lots of animals migrate back and forth between a summer home and a winter home. Animals are born knowing how to migrate. They also know where to go, even the first year when they have never been there before! Most animals begin to migrate in the late summer and early fall.

Some seabirds travel thousands of miles when they migrate. Land snails migrate only a few yards.

Some animals migrate because colder weather means their food supply gets low. Other animals migrate because their bodies are not able to handle the cold of winter. In the spring, when the earth gets warmer and there is more food to eat, these animals return to their summer homes and have babies.

Just for laughs

Q: Why do birds fly south for the winter?

A: Because it's too far to walk.

Words 2 Know

Fahrenheit: a scale for measuring temperature, where water freezes at 32 degrees.

Celsius: another scale for measuring temperature, where water freezes at 0 degrees.

migrate: to travel to the same place at the same time each year.

hibernate: to go into a deep sleep for many months with low body temperature and heart rate.

adapt: to make changes or to cope with your environment.

altitude: how high something is, measured above sea level.

You might think that every migrating animal in the Northern Hemisphere travels south for the winter. That is usually what happens, but not always! Animals such as Dall sheep live high in the mountains during the summer months when there is plenty of alpine grass there for them to eat. But when the winter snows come to the mountains and their food supply dies, these sheep move down the mountain to a lower **altitude** where there is less snow and more vegetation. So they don't migrate south, they migrate lower.

How Far Can You Go?

Why do some animals migrate so far, and some stay so close to home? This activity will help you think about why different kinds of animals travel different distances when they migrate. For this activity you will need a few people: one to call out animal names, and the others to be migrating animals.

1 Make a list of animals that move in different ways. You can include a bird that flies, a snake that slithers, a lobster that crawls backwards, and a deer that runs.

2 Decide how a human can best imitate how each of the animals on your list moves. Have everyone practice moving like each of the different animals.

3 Mark a starting point. This mark is the summer home of your animal, and where the racers will start their fall migration.

4 Measure about 25 meters or yards from the starting point. Mark that point. That is the finish line, and the winter home of your animal.

Supplies

list of migrating animals

measuring tape

an open area like a hallway, playground, or your back yard

stopwatch

5 Choose someone to be the caller. They will call out "ready, set," and then the name of a migrating animal instead of "go."

6 The racers must then begin migrating from the start to the finish using that animal's form of movement. If you are a goose, you can fly. If you are a snake, you must slither. If you are a whale, you must swim. If you are a lobster, you must crawl. If you are a deer, you can run or walk. While the racers are migrating, the caller can shout out a new animal, and the racers all change how they move to match that new animal.

7 Another fun variation on this activity is to use a stopwatch to time how long it takes each animal to migrate from its winter home to its summer home.

Things to notice

❅ Which animals were able to move fastest?

❅ Which animals were slowest?

❅ Is migration easy for all animals?

❅ What affects how far an animal can migrate?

Hibernation is a way some animals survive winter.

In winter it is hard for animals to find enough food.

Since sleeping takes up less energy than being awake, some animals go in a deep sleep during winter.

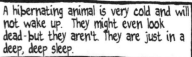

A hibernating animal is very cold and will not wake up. They might even look dead—but they aren't. They are just in a deep, deep sleep.

Some Animals Hibernate

The biggest problem for animals in winter is that it is hard to find food. Sure it's cold, but the real problem is finding enough to eat. Sleeping takes up less energy than being awake. Many animals go into a very deep sleep, sometimes for weeks or months at a time. This is hibernation. To hibernate means to go into such a deep sleep that the animal doesn't need to eat, drink, or even go to the bathroom. The animal's body temperature drops, sometimes as low as the air around it. Its heart rate drops to only a few beats a minute. It uses much less energy this way. A hibernating animal is very cold and will not wake up. It might even look dead—but it isn't. It is just in a deep, deep sleep.

WOW!

These animals all sleep through the winter: raccoons, skunks, woodchucks, chipmunks, hamsters, hedgehogs, bats, bears, platypuses, badgers, opossums, and koala bears.

Bears Sleep All Winter But Are Not Real Hibernators

When people think of hibernating animals, they usually think of bears. Bears can go up to 100 days without eating, drinking, peeing, or pooping. That's more than three months! But bears are not true hibernators because their body temperature doesn't really drop and they wake up pretty easily. Bears may wake up off and on during the winter, but when they are asleep, they are really asleep! They sleep so deeply that mother bears will have babies while they are sleeping in the winter.

Bears spend most of the summer and early fall eating as much as possible. They can gain as much as 30 pounds a week during the summer. All of the weight they gain keeps them warm all winter. That's why their temperatures don't drop very much, even when it's really cold.

Bears choose dens that are just barely big enough for them to move in. If a mother bear has cubs, they will all squeeze into the same den. Bears usually make dens in burrows, caves, hollowed-out trees, and rock  crevices. The entrances to these dens are small—just big enough for the bear to really squish itself inside. The insides of most bear dens are only about five feet wide and three feet high. It would be like living inside a refrigerator box!

Bears use the summer to get their winter dens ready. A mother bear and her cubs will bring leaves, grass, bark, and twigs into a den to make a cozy nest for winter. By the time late fall comes, the bears are fat, tired, and ready to sleep.

Many animals wake a few times during the winter months. If its body temperature gets too cold, it will start to shiver and wake up. This usually happens when the temperature outside goes much lower than usual. The animal might go deeper into its den to get a little warmer, then go right back to sleep.

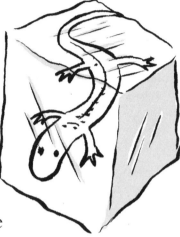

But even hibernating animals need fuel to keep their bodies going. How do they keep their bodies going if they sleep all winter long? Small sleepers, like squirrels, chipmunks, and mice, store food in their burrow. They wake up off and on throughout the winter and have something to eat. This keeps their body temperature from going too low. Many mammals get ready for the winter season by eating as much food as possible in the late summer and fall. They gain heavy layers of fat that insulate them against the cold. That fat also helps feed the animal's body as it sleeps.

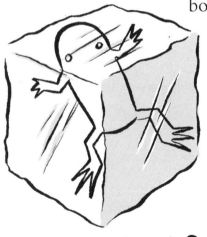

Some animals hibernate because their bodies can't cope with cold temperatures. Reptiles and amphibians don't produce their own body heat the way we do. They rely on the sun and warm temperatures to give their bodies heat. These animals are cold-blooded. Their blood isn't really cold, but cold-blooded animals need to be warm to move around, eat, and

WOW! Some amphibians, like the wood frog, freeze solid underneath leaves on the forest floor. They come back to life after the early spring rains thaw them out!

protect themselves. When it's cold, everything about these animals slows down, including their heart and lungs. They can't move. They can't eat. They can't even breathe.

When winter comes and the temperature is too cold for reptiles to keep warm, they **brumate**. This is the word for reptile hibernation. Turtles that live in water bury themselves in mud and leaves at the bottom of ponds or lakes, and let their bodies grow cold. They don't need to eat because their body systems are moving so slowly. Their hearts beat only once every few minutes. They don't need much oxygen because their lungs shut down. Instead, water turtles absorb tiny amounts of oxygen from the pond water through special skin cells on their tails. Turtles can brumate for several months.

Land reptiles such as snakes and land

Words 2 Know

brumate: reptile hibernation.

predator: an animal that preys on other animals.

torpor: a state of inactivity like a deep sleep.

dormant: resting and inactive.

diapause: a period of time when insects stop growing or changing.

larvae: the wormlike stage of an insect's life.

pupae: the cocoon stage of an insect's life when it changes from one form to another.

turtles brumate in burrows. Turtles dig their own burrows in the ground. Snakes find burrows used by other animals to curl up in. Brumating reptiles like snakes and turtles can't protect themselves from **predators**. It's too cold for them to move. A deep, safe burrow is their protection.

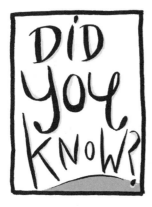

The common poorwill is the only bird known to hibernate. It lives in the California deserts. When food is scarce and temperatures are low, poorwills will go into a deep sleep, called **torpor**. The poorwills can stay in hibernation for several weeks at a time.

You won't find many insects hopping or flying around outside in the winter. That's because most insects are **dormant** or in **diapause** in the winter. This means that they stop growing and developing—in fact, they "pause." Their breathing, heartbeat, and temperature drop very low. Insects stay in diapause until the warm temperatures and sunlight of spring help them start to grow again. Some insects stay as **larvae** (their wormlike state) during the winter. Other insects are in their **pupae** stage. This is the stage when insects change from one form to another. Still other insects lay their eggs and die before winter begins. The eggs stay dormant all winter and hatch in the spring. Insects usually burrow deep into holes in the ground, in hollow logs, or under the bark of trees.

Build a Hibernation Den

Hibernating animals need to choose carefully where they will spend their winter sleep. They need a small space because their body heat must keep the space warm while they are asleep. They need a comfortable place that is safe from bad weather and predators. In this activity you will create a den that you would like to hibernate in.

Find a place to put your cardboard box where you will be safe from bad weather and predators, and stay hidden from any other danger. Use your blanket and pillow to create a cozy space to curl up into. Try out your den.

Supplies

cardboard box just big enough to fit inside

blankets and pillows

other "hibernating" supplies like a special stuffed animal, a book, a flashlight

Things to notice or think about

❈ What other supplies would a hibernating animal need or want?

❈ Would an animal need anything else?

❈ What different supplies would a human need or want? Why?

Plants Hibernate Too

Plants and trees make their own food energy from the sun. When it's cold and the sun's rays aren't direct enough for plants to make energy, the plants shut down. Their leaves die and drop off. The plants aren't dead, though. They are dormant. That means they are alive, but resting.

How do they stay alive? Right before plants go dormant in the fall, they store lots of sugar and salt in their roots. Sugar and salt gets in the way of ice forming in the plant's roots. You'll learn more about this in chapter 4. That helps the plant avoid ice damage. In the spring, more sun and warmer ground temperatures signal to the plants and leafy trees that it is time to wake up and get growing!

Deciduous Trees and Coniferous Trees

Deciduous trees usually have broad leaves that die and fall off in the fall. In the spring they grow new leaves. Deciduous trees like oak, birch, and maple grow in the temperate latitudes. Remember where this is? In between the tropics and the polar regions. But there are also deciduous trees closer to the equator, like teak and bamboo. They lose their leaves during the dry season.

Evergreen trees keep their leaves all year. Most evergreen trees in the temperate areas and polar regions are called **coniferous** trees. They usually have leaves shaped like needles and produce cones. Spruce trees and pine trees are conifers. Redwoods are probably the most famous.

Conifers grow everywhere that trees grow, but they are especially dominant in the coldest regions. The needles of conifers are just leaves that have adapted to cold climates! You know what else? The needles help keep these trees warm in the winter. Another way that these trees protect themselves from the winter weather is to grow close together. And have you ever noticed the way pine trees and other conifers are shaped like a cone at the top? This protects them from breaking under the weight of heavy snow. The snow can't pile up too high because it will slide off, just like it slides off a steep roof.

SUMMER FALL WINTER SPRING

Some Animals Adapt

Animals that don't hibernate or migrate have found ways to adapt to the cold. There are lots of animals you might find outside your door during the winter! They stay active and have evolved special ways to keep their bodies warm.

When you go outside to play in the winter, you probably wear a coat to keep warm. Why does your coat keep you warm when it is cold outside? Because it has extra layers inside it to hold in heat. Those extra layers are called insulation. Your coat might have a layer of fabric as insulation. It might have a layer of feathers as insulation. Both help to keep your body warmer because that extra layer holds your body heat in close to you. The heat from your body does not escape.

That's how animals stay warm, too. Birds have feathers. Mammals have fur or hair. Both feathers and fur help trap an animal's body heat close to its body. Its insulation keeps it warm and cozy.

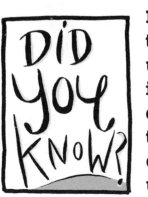

DID YOU KNOW?

Most mammals have two layers of fur. The underlayer is what insulates animals. The outerlayer protects them. When it gets cold out, the mammal's underlayer of fur puffs up a little bit. This traps still air and keeps the mammal warm. When you feel cold and get goosebumps, the hair on your body does the same thing that the underlayer of fur does. It puffs up to try to keep you warmer!

How Warm is Your Form?

Do you think dirt or fabric is better for insulation? What about a layer of paper? Here's an experiment that will help you find out what kinds of materials make good insulation. If you are trying this experiment when the weather is warm outside or you live in a place that just doesn't get cold, you can put the jars in the freezer instead of outside.

1 Write down the list of insulating materials you will be testing in your science journal. Use the supply list or think of your own.

2 You'll be testing two jars at a time. Fill all the baby food jars with water. The water in all the jars should be around or close to the same temperature. It's important that the water is room temperature already so it won't change until you put the jars outside. Measure the temperature of the water in each jar. Record this in your science journal. Screw on the jar lids and place two jars on the tray.

3 Make sure the jars are far enough away from each other so that the insulating material for one jar doesn't affect another jar.

4 Wrap or surround each baby food jar with a different kind of insulating material. For example, you can put one jar in a wool sock. You can pile Styrofoam packing material all around another.

5 Carry the tray outside or put it in the freezer. Leave the jars for ten minutes. Meanwhile prepare two more jars, put them on a new tray, and bring them out when the first pair is ready to come in.

6 Bring the first two jars back inside, unscrew the lids, and measure the temperature of the water in each. Record the temperature in your science journal next to it on the materials list. You can repeat this experiment with different materials, or try leaving the jars out in the cold for longer. Test one jar completely uncovered so you know how cold an uninsulated jar will be. This is called a "control" in an experiment.

Things to notice

* Which insulating material kept the water in the jars the warmest?

* Which insulating material let the water in the jars cool down the most?

* Which insulating material was the easiest to wrap around the jar?

* Which insulating material was the hardest to wrap around the jar?

* What else did you notice about this experiment?

Supplies

science journal

about 10 baby food jars with lids

gallon jug of water at room temperature

good thermometer

several trays

down jacket

cotton sock

wool sock

gloves of any material

mittens of any material

other types of cloth or clothing

Styrofoam or packing peanuts

dirt

large piece of paper

aluminum foil

ziplock plastic bag

leaves

Feathers are really all warm!

Did you ever wonder how ducks can stay warm in icy water? It's all in their feathers! Bird feathers are waterproof. They hold in body heat and keep out water. But guess what happens when there is an oil spill and birds get oil on their feathers? This experiment will show you how well feathers can keep birds warm. It will also show you what happens when feathers get coated with oil, such as when a seabird lands in an oil slick on the ocean.

1 Put the ice cubes in one of the baggies and close it tight. Put the feathers in one of the other baggies and close it tight.

2 Put the empty baggie in the palm of your hand. Now put the baggie full of ice on your hand. Count how long the baggie is on your hand before your hand becomes cold. Take off the ice-filled baggie and the empty baggie. Record this data in your science journal.

Supplies
ice cubes

3 ziplock plastic baggies

feathers from any craft store

vegetable oil

old paintbrush

science journal

3 Put the feather-filled baggie in the palm of your hand. Now put the baggie full of ice on your hand. Count how long the baggie is on your hand before your hand becomes cold. Record this data.

4 Open the baggie with the feathers in it. Brush some oil onto the feathers with the paintbrush, then close the bag again.

5 Put the feather-filled baggie in the palm of your hand. Now put the baggie full of ice on your hand. Count how long the baggie is on your hand before your hand becomes cold.

DID YOU KNOW?

Bird feathers are made of keratin, which is the same stuff that makes up your hair and fingernails!

Things to notice

❉ How long did it take for you to feel the cold with the plain baggie?

❉ How long did it take for you to feel the cold with the baggie of feathers?

❉ How long did it take for you to feel the cold with the baggie of oil-coated feathers?

❉ What do you think happened to the feathers when oil got on them?

❉ What else did you notice with this experiment?

Why Oil Spills Are Bad for Seabirds

You will probably see that when oil gets on feathers, they get all gooey and wet—and they stay that way. They aren't fluffy anymore. They are just matted and heavy. Without fluffy, dry feathers, seabirds can't stay warm. When their feathers are heavy, they can't fly. That's what happens when seabirds get coated in oil from oil spills. When rescuers find seabirds with feathers coated in oil, they wash them with detergent and water to get the oil out.

Fat Is Where It's At

Some animals use fat to keep their bodies warm. Mammals that live in cold water, like whales, seals, and porpoises, have a very thick layer of fat just under their skin. It protects the animal's insides from getting too cold in the icy water. Here's a way to find out how fat works to insulate.

1 Coat one of your index fingers with petroleum jelly. This is like covering your finger in a layer of fat.

2 Stick both of your index fingers into the bowl of cold water for two minutes.

Things to notice

❊ How does the water feel on the finger covered in "fat?"

❊ Which finger feels warmer in the water?

Supplies
petroleum jelly
ice water

Keeping Warm

How do you stay warm? The next time you are outside think of all the ways an animal might stay warm. Try these out!

❊ Curl up in a ball. Does it matter what surface you lie on?

❊ Be very active—try running around a lot to keep moving.

❊ Stay very still. Try facing the wind. Try being still with your back to the wind.

❊ Huddle together as a group. Try this with one other person, two or three people, and as a large group.

❊ Find a place out of the wind. Stand behind a building. Stand in a group of trees.

Which method of keeping warm worked best for you? Was there a method that didn't work for you? Which method of keeping warm used up the most energy? What would happen when you got tired? Which method of keeping warm used up the least energy?

Adapting to the Winter Environment

You already know that many animals have a hard time finding food in the winter. Some animals travel to warmer places to find enough to eat. Other animals sleep away the cold winter days so they don't have to eat at all.

But how do animals find enough to eat if they don't migrate or hibernate? They adapt, or change in some way, to be able to find food and safe shelter in the cold winter months.

Animals that stick around get the first pick of habitat. The ones that don't hibernate or migrate get their choice when it comes time to make nests and have babies in the spring. They are the first animals in a habitat when nesting season comes. Hibernating and migrating creatures have to choose from whatever is left over!

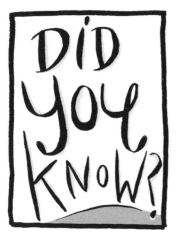

It Depends on Their Environment

Animals' bodies adapt to winter in many ways. Some animals have bodies that are designed to work well in snow. Have you ever tried to walk on top of the snow but sink down up to your knees? That's because your feet aren't very big compared to the size of your body. Animals often have the same problem. Picture the long, skinny legs and small, hooved feet of deer. Deer have a very hard time walking through deep snow. Their small feet can't hold their bodies on top.

But some animals find it easy to walk on the snow. Lynx and snowshoe hares grow extra hair on their feet so it is easier for them to move fast on top of the snow. Their feet are very large and wide compared to the rest of their body. They can almost float on top of the snow without punching through.

Just for laughs

Q: What did the little bird say to the big bird?

A: Peck on someone your own size.

Birds also can stay on top of the snow easily. Birds' bodies are very light, because their bones are hollow. They don't put much weight on the snow to begin with. But there are some pretty big birds out there. How do wild turkeys, raptors, and vultures keep from sinking into the snow? Birds have long, clawed feet that spread out over a wide surface. Those skinny feet act like a tripod. They spread the bird's weight over a broad area. No spot pushes down into the snow more than another.

WOW!

Some birds have built-in feet heaters! Birds have skinny little legs and feet, but their feet don't seem to get too cold, even when the weather is icy. Here's why. Some birds are built so that the blood vessels going from their heart to their feet are right next to the blood vessels coming from their feet to their heart. Warm blood coming from the bird's heart to its feet helps warm up the cooler blood moving from its feet to its heart. The bird loses less body heat and keeps its legs and feet nice and toasty—it's like having a built in foot warmer!

Make Snow (or Sand) Shoes!

Have you ever tried to walk on snow using snowshoes? Snowshoes work the same way that a snowshoe hare's feet work. They spread your body weight over a wider area. This lets you "float" on top of the snow. In this activity you'll make a simple pair of snow or sand shoes. If you live in a place that doesn't get snow, you can try this activity in a sandbox. Your snow (sand) shoes will show you how much easier it is to push on a soft surface like snow or sand if you can cover more of the surface.

Ask a grownup for help with the scissors.

1 Use the marker to trace about five inches around each foot. The drawing should look a bit like big ovals.

2 Make a mark on the cardboard on each side of your foot where your shoelaces tie. This is where you will attach your laces.

Supplies

heavy cardboard like an old pizza box

pencil or marker

scissors

2 large heavy-duty rubber bands or 4 pieces of twine or heavy string

stapler

3 Cut out the shapes with the scissors. Cut each heavy-duty rubber band so it is one long rubber string.

4 Staple the rubber band onto the cardboard shapes where you made the mark on either side of your foot. Leave enough slack so you can put your foot in. If you use string or twine, staple one piece of twine to each mark.

5 Slide your foot under the rubber band. If you are using twine, tie your snowshoes on to your feet. Try them out!

Things to notice

❊ Did you have to change the way you walk with snowshoes? How?

❊ Did you try your snowshoes on snow or sand?

❊ Why is it easier to walk on snow or sand with snowshoes than with just your feet?

Hiding in Plain Sight

One of the most important ways some animals adapt to winter is to change the way they look. This is called **camouflage**. Animals use it to stay safe.

You may notice that most animals have fur or feathers that blend in very well with their environments. Most mammals have brown, gray, or black fur. Many birds have brown and gray colors on their wings. These colors help animals blend in with the colors of leaves, bark, and grasses. But if it snows, brown, gray, and black fur will show up very well. That's why many animals that don't hibernate in winter actually change color so they can be outside and still be safe. Snowshoe hares, ermine, and arctic foxes all change from showing a dark brown coat to a pure white coat. They can stay hidden right out on the snowy ground.

43

Sneak Camouflage Peek

How well do you think you could spot an animal that has camouflaged itself through its color? Here's your chance! This activity works whether you have snow or not. It will show you just how well animals can hide when they blend into their surroundings. This activity works best if you have two or more people. One person places the camouflage shapes. The others find them.

1 Trace around the cookie cutters on both the brown and white pieces of paper. Make lots of shapes. Cut out all of your animals.

2 One person takes the cut-out animals and places them outside. Place some of the brown shapes in places where there is lots of brown bark or leaves or dirt. Place at least one of the brown shapes where there is no other brown coloring.

3 If you have snow, place at least one of the brown animal shapes on the snow. Take the white animals and place some of them in places where there is either snow or a very light-colored background. Place at least one of the white animals on a very dark background.

4 Now have the other person go outside and try to find all of the animals.

Things to notice

❋ Which animals were easiest to find? Why?

❋ Which animals were hardest to find? Why?

Supplies

cookie cutters in the shapes of animals

pencil

4 sheets of brown construction paper

4 sheets of white construction paper

scissors

44

Inside Camouflage Hide!

This activity is also fun indoors. It will help you see how animals can hide in plain sight in every environment.

1 Trace around the cookie cutters on the different pieces of paper. Make lots of animal shapes. Cut out all of your animals.

2 One person takes the shapes and places or tapes them on backgrounds that are the same color or similar. If you have a green animal, place it on a green plant leaf. If you have a pink animal, place it on a pink book cover or a pink jacket. Then have your partner try to find all of your animals.

Things to notice

❊ What made it easy to find the animals?

❊ What made it hard to find the animals?

❊ What does this activity help tell you about how animals use colors to hide?

Supplies

cookie cutters in the shapes of animals

pencil

6 sheets of construction paper of different colors

scissors

tape

45

Animals Change the Menu

Another way animals can adapt to winter is to change what they eat. Many animals change their diets when their favorite food is not available. In many places in winter, there are not very many different kinds of food around. For example, animals that eat grasses or other green plants need to find something else to eat when the grasses die or are covered in snow. Animals like deer and moose eat berries, twigs, and branches in the winter, when there aren't any other plants.

Animals that hunt and eat other animals have to change their diets in winter, too. Sometimes this is because their **prey** isn't around in the winter. A lot of animals sleep through winter so they can be hard to find. Sometimes **predators** need to change their diets

Words 2 Know

camouflage: to hide by changing the way you look.

prey: animals that get eaten by predators.

because they can't hunt their food the same way in winter that they do in the summer. Coyotes like to hunt and eat snowshoe hares. But in winters with deep snow, coyotes can't catch the snowshoe hares. The coyotes can't run on the top of the snow as quickly as the hares can. Coyotes will change their diet and eat small mice or other creatures that tunnel just under the snow instead. These animals are easier to catch.

Lots of birds eat insects and fruit and worms during the spring, summer, and fall. But most insects are hard to find in the winter. Worms are frozen in the ground! So what do these birds do? They change the menu! Birds eat insects for their protein. When the insects go away, the birds find other sources of protein—like seeds!

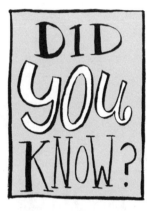

Perennial plants survive the winter and grow new leaves and flowers each spring. Annual plants die each winter and have to start again from new seeds in the spring.

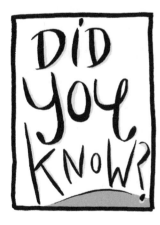

You can tell what a bird likes to eat best—and how they get it—by its beak. Birds that eat mostly seeds, like cardinals, finches, and sparrows, have short, powerful beaks. They use their beaks to crack open seeds. Birds with long, pointed beaks, like woodpeckers, bore holes in trees to catch insects. Birds like swallows, warblers, and wrens have small bills that can open wide for catching and eating insects.

Build a Bird Food Tracker

Supplies

aluminum pie plates
sunflower seeds
hammer and nails
pine cones
string
butter knife
peanut butter
millet
mixed bird seed
shallow bowl or dish
an orange, cut in half
scissors
science journal

One interesting way to learn what kinds of foods different birds prefer is to track their eating habits. Set up some bird feeders with different kinds of food. You can watch to see which birds like which kinds.

You can make some easy bird feeders to hang outside and track the birds. Here are the different kinds of feeders to try. Make two of each kind. Have a grownup help you with the hammer and scissors.

Think carefully about where your feeders will go. If you can see them all from the same window or other spot you'll have more fun with this project.

Pie pan feeder

Place a pie pan with sunflower seeds on a flat spot in your yard. Put another one a little higher—maybe nail it to a post or wedge it in the crotch of a tree. Make sure you empty out the pie pan after it rains or snows and add fresh seeds.

Pine cone feeder

Tie a long string around the top of each pine cone. You will use the string to hang the feeder on a tree or post. Spread peanut butter all over each pine cone to really coat them. Pour mixed bird seed or millet in the shallow dish. Roll the pine cones in the seeds. The seeds will stick to the peanut butter. Hang one pine cone feeder from a post or tree branch, and find a place to hang the other one slightly closer to the ground.

Orange feeder

Use the scissors to poke a hole through the middle of each orange half. Take long pieces of string and thread them through the oranges. Tie the string so each orange hangs like an ornament. Hang one orange feeder from a post or tree branch and find a place to hang the other one slightly closer to the ground.

Now that you have your feeders in place, watch the birds eat. Use your science journal to record which kinds of birds like which kinds of food. You can make a chart.

low sunflower
high sunflower
low peanut butter
high peanut butter
low orange
high orange

Things to Notice

❋ What kinds of birds liked which kinds of food?

❋ Do different birds like to eat at a certain height above the ground?

❋ Do some birds always stay on the ground?

❋ Do some birds eat more than one food?

❋ Do some birds eat at the same time every day?

Look What's on the Menu

The next time you take a walk outside, look carefully around for signs that animals have been eating close by. Write down in your science journal some signs that might show that an animal was having a bite to eat.

Things to Notice

❋ Nipped twigs where you would expect to find a leaf bud at the end of a small twig. This could mean deer have been eating buds.

❋ Crushed acorns, or acorns with teeth marks on them. This could mean deer have been eating them. They enjoy the meat inside the nut, but will leave the crushed, outer shells on the ground.

❋ Piles of pine cones with all the seeds chewed off. This could mean squirrels and chipmunks have been eating them.

❋ Bark off trees and branches in strips. This could mean a porcupine has been chewing on the tree.

❋ Wood chips at the base of trees. This could mean large woodpeckers are drilling for insects.

Supplies

science journal
pen or pencil

Water and Ice— How Nice!

Chapter 4

What is cold and frozen and melts in your mouth? **Ice!** In many places on earth, ice is a big part of winter. Ice is water. So is snow. So are rain and hail and sleet and fog and mist.

It's all water in different forms, and it is all part of the **water cycle**. What is the water cycle? Well, water covers almost three-fourths of the earth. The sun's heat is constantly making some of that water

evaporate from the surface of the oceans, lakes, and rivers. What happens when water evaporates? It turns into **water vapor**. That water vapor rises as warm, humid air. When water vapor reaches cooler air, it cools too, and **condenses** into clouds of liquid droplets. These droplets combine and grow until they get heavy and fall to the earth as **precipitation**. This can be as rain, snow, sleet, or hail.

The water falls on the ground, and into the lakes and oceans. Then the sun's heat makes some of that water evaporate and the process starts all over again. The water cycle happens every day of every year, all over earth. There really isn't a beginning or an end. Every part of the water cycle is happening all the time.

In winter, if it's cold, the water vapor that condenses into clouds forms crystals of ice. Why does this happen? Because of the sun.

Words 2 Know

ice: the solid state of water.

water cycle: the continuous movement of water from the earth to the clouds and back to earth again.

evaporate: to change from the liquid state to the gas or vapor state of water.

water vapor: the gas state of water.

condense: to move from the gas state to the liquid state of water.

precipitation: rain, snow, sleet, or hail.

WOW!

Only 2 percent of all the water on earth is fresh water. That's the same as if you had 100 bathtubs full of water, and 98 would be full of salt water and only 2 would be full of fresh water.

Remember that in northern climates the sun hits the earth at an angle in winter. Both the ground and air have cooled down. The sun's heat still evaporates water from the oceans, but the temperature of the air above the ground is cold.

As water vapor rises it meets very cold air above. That cold air turns the water vapor into ice crystals. Just like rain, ice crystals fall from the clouds when the clouds get so heavy with moisture that they can't hold it any more. If the air temperature is warm enough the crystals might melt on their way down and fall as rain. But if it's cold enough the crystals won't melt and they'll fall as snowflakes. If the ground is frozen, the frozen crystals pile up on top of each other. The snow can get really deep!

Just for laughs

Q: Why is a polar bear cheap to have as a pet?

A: It lives on ice!

The Four Parts of the Water Cycle

Evaporation: the sun's heat turns water into water vapor.

Condensation: the water vapor rises into the air, cools, and condenses into clouds of liquid droplets or ice crystals.

Precipitation: condensed water vapor falls to the earth's surface as rain or snow.

Saturation: the water falling on land collects in rivers and lakes, soil and porous layers of rock, and much of it flows back into the ocean.

DID YOU KNOW?

The water you drink every day and the snow and rain that falls from the sky has been around on planet Earth since the days of the dinosaurs! The same water keeps going around and around in the water cycle. That's why it's so important to take care of our water and keep it clean. It's the only water we have!

When Water Freezes, It Expands

Just like cold air is heavier than warm air, cold water is heavier than warm water. Cold water sinks. Warm water rises. That's why when you jump into a lake or pond in the summer, the water is colder deeper down. The colder water sinks below the warmer water.

But what is amazing about fresh water is that when it freezes, it floats. Why? Because ice is not as heavy as water. Water **expands** when it freezes into ice. The liquid turns into crystals that attach to each other in a lattice pattern. Those crystals spread out. They take up more space, but they don't get any heavier.

Just for laughs

Q: Why do seals swim in salt water?

A: Because pepper water makes them sneeze!

AACHOO

WOW! Almost 90 percent of the world's ice is in Antarctica. The ice there measures 7,000 feet thick. Inside that ice is almost 70 percent of all the fresh water on earth. If the world contained 100 bathtubs of fresh water, 70 would be in Antarctica and 30 would be everywhere else. Antarctica is pretty important!

You can see how water expands by looking at how puddles freeze from the outside in. That's because the shallow water is on the edges of the puddle. The deeper water is in the middle. Sometimes you can see ridged rings covering the ice over a puddle. Those ridged rings happen because the water on the outside surface of the puddle freezes first. Then some water closer to the center of the puddle freezes, expands, and pushes right over the top of the old ice and causes a ridge. Water even closer to the center of the puddle freezes and pushes over the top of the other ridge. And so on, until the whole puddle is frozen.

At What Temperature Does Water Freeze?

It depends on how you measure temperature. Fahrenheit and Celsius are different ways to measure temperature. They are named after the people who invented them. Celsius temperatures are based on the metric system, which measures by units of 10. On the Celsius scale, water freezes at 0 degrees and boils at 100 degrees. In the Fahrenheit scale, water freezes at 32 degrees and boils at 212 degrees. Fahrenheit temperatures are based on a scale of 180 degrees (212 degrees minus 32 degrees equals 180). Most countries and all scientists use the Celsius scale now. Here is a chart that tells you what a temperature in Fahrenheit equals in Celsius.

212 degrees Fahrenheit = 100 degrees Celsius (water boils)

77 degrees Fahrenheit = 25 degrees Celsius

32 degrees Fahrenheit = 0 degrees Celsius (water freezes)

0 degrees Fahrenheit = minus 17.8 degrees Celsius

WOW!

Most cities use salt to melt snow and ice on their roads in winter because it is cheap and easy to find. But many substances dissolved in water will keep the water from freezing at cold temperatures. Maybe cities could spread big bags of sugar on the road to keep cars from slipping. Mmm!

If you have ever gone ice skating or slid on some ice, you know that ice is really, really slippery. Why is that? Some scientists think it has to do with the way ice crystals behave. The teeny tiny particles that make up the outside surface of ice move back and forth very, very fast. These particles are called **molecules**. The molecules on the surface move quickly because there are no molecules above them to help hold them in place. So why isn't solid wood slippery on its surface? The molecules of ice crystals **vibrate** faster than the molecules of any other solid. So even though ice is solid water, the very top layer of the ice doesn't act like a solid. It acts like a liquid. If you try to walk on it, that ice layer under your foot behaves like a liquid and so your foot slides. The colder the ice gets, the stickier it gets—so it becomes easier to walk on.

Words 2 Know

expand: to increase in size or to take up more space.

molecule: the tiniest particles that make up objects.

vibrate: to move back and forth very, very quickly.

density: the mass of something compared to how much space it takes up. A bucket of sand will be more dense than a bucket of feathers. A solid object is more dense than an object with lots of holes in it. Ice is less dense than liquid water—that's why ice floats.

solution: one substance dissolved into another.

Make Ice Spikes

Want to see expanding ice in action? Sometimes the surface of water can freeze so quickly that the water underneath has no place to go but up. This can happen in an ice cube tray. When surface water freezes very quickly it can leave a small hole. The water underneath the surface pushes up through the hole and freezes, bit by bit, into a hollow spike. Finally the hole in the main ice cube freezes and the spike stays on top of the cube. Here is a way you can try to grow some ice spikes in your own freezer. If you use distilled water you will get better results. Distilled water is water that has no minerals in it.

Pour the distilled water into the ice cube trays and put the trays in the freezer. Wait several hours. You should notice some very cool ice spikes.

Supplies

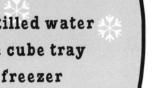

distilled water
ice cube tray
freezer

Have you ever looked into the sky and seen a ring or halo around the sun or moon? Some people call these sun dogs and moon dogs. These rings aren't really rings (or dogs) at all. When sunlight or moonlight shines through a very thin layer of ice crystals high up in the sky, the ice crystals work just like a camera lens. They bend the light into a halo, or circle, around the sun or moon. Moon dogs are rare because the moon has to be quite bright for a moon dog—so it has to be close to a full moon.

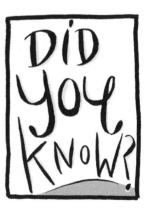

DID YOU KNOW?

Water is Dense!

In this activity you'll be able to see how cold water is denser than warm water—but ice isn't dense at all!

1 Add food coloring to a pitcher of water. Pour the water into ice cube trays and freeze.

2 Fill the water glasses about halfway full of plain water. Add one or two ice cubes to each glass. Now watch what happens.

❄ Supplies ❄

pitcher

water

blue or green food coloring

ice cube tray

2 or 3 water glasses

Things to Notice

❀ Did the ice sink or float?

❀ Where did the food coloring go as the ice melted?

❀ After doing this experiment what do you think about the density of cold water compared to the density of warm water?

Salt Water is Really Dense!

In this activity you can compare the **density** of salt water, fresh water, ice, and corn oil. The more dense liquid will sink to the bottom, while the less dense liquid will rise to the top.

1 Pour one-half cup of salt into one cup of water. Stir until the salt dissolves into the water. Add a few drops of food coloring and stir the **solution** some more. Pour your solution into a tall glass to fill it about one-third full. This is glass number one.

2 Pour a cup of plain water into another glass. Add a few drops of a different color food coloring and stir it up. This is glass number two.

3 Very carefully and slowly pour some of the water from glass number two into glass number one so that glass number one is two-thirds full. If you pour it in carefully, the salt water should stay on the bottom and the fresh water will sit on top, since salt water is more dense then fresh water.

4 Add corn oil to glass number one. How dense is the corn oil compared to the salt water and the fresh water? Does it sit on top? If it does, that means corn oil is less dense. Or does it sink to the bottom? If it sinks, it is more dense. What happens when you place an ice cube in the glass? Record your observations in your science journal.

Things to Notice

❄ What liquid is the most dense?

❄ What liquid is the least dense?

❄ What happens to the water in the ice cube as the ice cube melts?

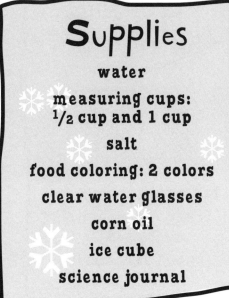

Supplies

water

❄ measuring cups: 1/2 cup and 1 cup

❄ salt

food coloring: 2 colors

clear water glasses

corn oil

ice cube

science journal

Amazing Salt Water Study

Everyone knows that water freezes at 32 degrees Fahrenheit (0 degrees Celsius), right? Well, not always! If you add salt to cold water, it has to get much colder to freeze. Salt water freezes at a much lower temperature—as low as about minus 6 degrees Fahrenheit (minus 21 degrees Celsius). Why? When salt is dissolved in water, the salt gets in the way of the ice crystals that are trying to form. The salt keeps the water in liquid form at colder temperatures. Here's a way to see how cold some water can get before it freezes if you add salt to it.

1 Fill a glass half full with water. Add a few ice cubes. Take the temperature of the ice water. Write the temperature down in your science journal.

2 Add some more ice cubes and take the temperature again. Write down the temperature in your science journal. What do you think will happen when you add more ice? Write your theory down in your science journal.

3 Stir one-half teaspoon of salt into your ice water solution. Add more ice. Record the temperature.

4 Keep adding salt to your solution, one-half teaspoon at a time. Be sure to stir each time so it dissolves, and keep checking the temperature.

Supplies

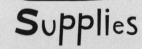

clear water glasses
water
ice cubes
thermometer
science journal
pencil
table salt or rock salt
teaspoon measuring spoon
spoon for stirring

Things to Notice

❄ What was the lowest temperature you wrote down?

❄ How much salt did you put in the water?

❄ Did adding extra ice cubes lower the water temperature?

Make Ice Cream!

Ice cream is a combination of sugar, milk, and flavorings. Mixed together these will not freeze at 32 degrees Fahrenheit (0 degrees Celsius). To make ice cream you need to put the mixture in a container surrounded by a solution colder that 32 degrees Fahrenheit. In this activity, you'll use salt's amazing ability to chill out to make a tasty treat.

1 Mix the sugar, milk, and vanilla together in the small bag. Zip it tight. Put the small bag inside the big plastic bag. Add the rock salt and the ice cubes to the large plastic bag, then zip it shut.

2 Shake and roll the big bag over and over, until the mixture in the inner bag is frozen. This might take about 20 minutes.

Things to notice

The mixture of ice and salt will melt a bit from contact with your hands. But the salty water is cooled by the ice, so the temperature of the liquid is below the freezing point of pure water. The inner bag can make better contact with the salty water and ice mixture than it could with just ice.

Supplies

1 sandwich-sized plastic ziplock bag

1 tablespoon sugar

1 cup whole milk

1 teaspoon vanilla

1 gallon-sized plastic ziplock bag

2 tablespoons rock salt

enough ice cubes to almost fill the larger bag

All About Snow

Snow is amazing. You can scoop it up and pat it into snowballs. You can build forts out of it. You can play in it, and slide on top of it.

You can burrow underneath it. You can even eat it! But what exactly is snow, and how is it formed?

Snowflakes are not frozen raindrops. When raindrops freeze on their way to the ground, they fall as sleet. Snowflakes are ice crystals that have joined with other ice crystals.

Words 2 Know

hexagon: six-sided shape.

symmetrical: the same on all sides.

How a Snowflake Is Made

You've already learned all about the water cycle. You know how the sun's heat evaporates water so it rises as water vapor and condenses into clouds. In cold temperatures, water droplets in clouds freeze into tiny ice crystals with six sides. A six-sided shape is called a **hexagon**. These hexagonal ice crystals are the building blocks of snowflakes. Sometimes the hexagons are stubby and fat. Sometimes they are long and thin. There are seven different ice crystal shapes, but they are all six-sided. Ice crystals can have different shapes for many reasons. The temperature of the air, how high up in the sky they are when they crystallize, and how much moisture is in the air affect an ice crystal's shape.

Here's how the crystals become snowflakes: each ice crystal is surrounded by water vapor in the cloud. Those water droplets freeze, and attach to the ice crystal on one of its six sides. That makes the ice crystal grow branches off of its six sides. It turns into a snowflake.

WOW!

In 1921, at least 75 inches (193 centimeters) of snow fell in one day on Silver Lake, Colorado. That's over 6 feet (almost 2 meters)! It was the biggest snowfall ever recorded in a 24-hour period.

Make a Hexagonal Prism

Hexagons are the building blocks of snowflakes. They can be long and thin, short and stubby, or wide and flat, but they are always six-sided. This project will show you a three-dimensional view of how a snowflake starts.

1 Start with four marshmallows and four toothpicks. Attach them to make a square. Attach two toothpicks to the marshmallows on the top and bottom of the square. It will look a little bit like a ladder.

2 Attach marshmallows on the four ends of the toothpicks at the top and bottom of the ladder.

3 Take four more toothpicks and four more marshmallows. Attach them to make a square. Attach two toothpicks to the marshmallows on the top and bottom. This will make another ladder.

4 Now turn the first ladder on its side. Turn the second ladder on its side. Attach the toothpicks at the top and bottom of the second ladder to the marshmallows at the top and bottom of the first ladder. You will have to bend the ladders to make them fit. When you are done, you will have a six-sided shape—a hexagon! This is what an ice crystal looks like.

5 If you want to keep going and add branches to your ice crystal, you can add toothpicks and marshmallows to each of the six sides. You can use however many toothpicks and marshmallows you want. You can make the snowflakes **symmetrical**, which means that every side will look the same, but you don't have to. Most snowflakes aren't symmetrical—their six branches can look very different.

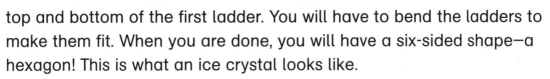

Every snowflake's branches are different from every other snowflake's branches. You could look at every snowflake that has ever fallen and still not find two that are exactly alike.

Collecting Snowflakes

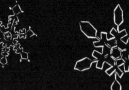

You need to live in a place where it snows to do this activity.

1 The next time it snows, take a piece of black paper outside—it is easier to see the snowflake's details when it is against a dark background.

2 Catch a few snowflakes on the paper. Use your magnifying glass to take a close look at the snowflakes.

Supplies

black paper
magnifying glass
snowflakes!

Snowflake Bentley

Wilson Bentley was the first person to photograph a snowflake. He lived in Vermont. His camera was attached to a microscope. He took photos of snowflakes by standing outside in the worst blizzards he could find. Wilson Bentley would catch a snowflake on a slide and put it under the microscope. After quickly focusing his camera before the snowflake could melt he'd take the picture and capture the snowflake's photo. Wilson Bentley photographed more than 5,000 different snowflakes. No two were exactly alike. He became so famous for his snowflake photographs, that he was known throughout America as Snowflake Bentley. You can read all about him in Jacqueline Briggs Martin's book, *Snowflake Bentley*.

Make Snowflake Fossils

This is a really fun way to preserve snowflakes so you can look at them long after they've melted.

1 Put the slides in the freezer so they won't melt the snowflakes when you collect them. Put the hairspray in an unheated garage or a place where it will be cold but not frozen solid.

2 The next time it snows, bring out the slides. Spray some hairspray on one side of the slide. Catch a snowflake on that sticky side of the slide.

3 Use the toothpick to gently move the snowflake to the middle of the slide. Carefully put the slide in a covered, cold place like an unheated garage and don't touch it for several hours. That will give the hairspray a chance to harden into the snowflake shape.

4 When the hairspray has hardened, you will have a perfect image of the snowflake to study. It will be easier to see if you look at it under a magnifying glass or a microscope.

Supplies

clear plastic microscope slides

hairspray—the aerosol spray kind, not the pump kind

snowflakes

toothpicks

magnifying glass or microscope

Growing Sugar Crystals

Snowflakes are six-sided crystals. Other crystals can have many different sides and shapes. In this activity you will grow sugar crystals. When the crystals form, you can look at them with a magnifying glass to see what shapes they are (and maybe take a taste!).

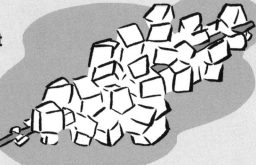

This activity uses boiling water so you will need a grownup to help you!

1 Boil the water, then add sugar a spoonful at a time to the boiling water. Stir to dissolve the sugar each time. When no more sugar will dissolve in the water it will sit on the bottom and won't disappear. Pour the sugar water into the glass jar.

2 Tie the piece of string to the middle of the pencil, then tie a paper clip to the end of the string. Lay the pencil across the top of the jar so the string hangs down into the sugar water and the paper clip is in the sugar water. Make sure the string doesn't hit the sides of the jar.

3 Put the jar in a sunny place. Check your jar every day to see what's happening. After one week, pull the string out of the jar.

Supplies

1 cup water

pan or bowl for boiling water and making solution

3 cups sugar

spoon or stirring rod

clean glass jar

pencil

string or yarn—crystals won't stick to nylon

paperclip

magnifying glass

science journal

Things to notice

❊ What happened to the level of sugar water in the jar?

❊ Did sugar crystals form on the string?

❊ What do the sugar crystals look like?

❊ Draw the shape of the sugar crystals in your science journal.

Growing Salt Crystals

This time let's grow salt crystals and see how they are different from sugar crystals.

1 Pour a cup of warm (not boiling) water into the glass jar. Stir the salt into the water a bit at a time until no more salt will dissolve in the water. When this happens the salt will sit on the bottom of the glass and won't disappear. Stir in a couple of drops of food coloring.

2 Tie the piece of string to the middle of the pencil, then tie a paper clip to the end of the string. Lay the pencil across the top of the jar so the string hangs down into the salt water and the paper clip almost touches the bottom.

3 Make sure the string doesn't touch the sides of the jar. Put the jar in a sunny place. Check your salt water jar every day. After one week, pull the string out of the jar.

Things to notice

❄ What happened to the level of salt water?

❄ Did salt crystals form on the string?

❄ How long did it take for salt crystals to form?

❄ Did the salt crystals form faster or slower than the sugar crystals?

❄ What do the salt crystals look like?

❄ How are salt crystals different from or the same as sugar crystals?

❄ Draw the shape of your crystals in your science journal.

Supplies

1 cup warm water
❄ clean glass jar
2 cups of salt
spoon or stirring rod
food coloring
pencil ❄
thread or string
❄ paperclip
science journal

Tropical Snow

You might think that if you live in the tropics, the part of the earth closest to the equator, you would never see snow. But that's not so! While there really isn't winter in the tropics because it gets almost the same amount of direct sunlight all year round, parts of the tropics do have snowy mountain peaks. Why? Because of the altitude, or height, of the mountains. Remember that snow forms because the air surrounding the clouds full of water droplets is cold. So the water droplets freeze into ice crystals. The ice crystals don't melt when they fall to the ground. Since air temperatures get colder the higher in the sky you go, high mountain peaks will have cold temperatures on top no matter where on earth they are located. Places like Hawaii and Kenya have very high mountain peaks. Hawaii's Mt. Haleakala, for example, is 10,200 feet high (3,100 meters). Kenya's Mt. Kilimanjaro is 19,000 feet high (5,800 meters). Snow falls on those mountain tops because the mountains are so high that the air surrounding them is quite cold. But lower down on the mountains the air is warm all year round.

Just for laughs

Q: What sort of ball doesn't bounce?

A: A snowball!

DID YOU KNOW?

Practically every part of the United States has had snow. Even most parts of southern Florida have had a few snow flurries at some time or other.

What Kind of Snow, Do You Know?

If you live in a place where it snows in the winter, you probably know that every snowfall is a little different. Sometimes the snow will be very heavy and easy to pack into snowballs. Other times the snow will fall in fine crystals, almost like sugar. It all depends on how much water is in the snow. The amount of water in any snowfall depends on lots of things, like temperature, location, air pressure, and altitude. Snow with more water in it is more **dense**. It is heavier than snow without much water in it.

When snow falls to the ground, it compresses, or gets squeezed. The air between the snowflakes gets pushed out and the snowflakes get pushed closer together. More snowflakes closer together means more water in the snow. So snow close to the ground is usually more dense than snow on top.

dense: packed tightly. Snow with more water in it is more dense than snow that is very dry.

Crazy Kinds of Skier Snow

Skiers love snow! Since they spend so much time on snow, skiers have made up all kinds of words for it. Their descriptions are based on the way the snow feels under their skis. Here are some.

Powder: light, fluffy snow that has just fallen.

Freshies: untracked, unskied, untouched powder.

Champagne powder: the lightest, fluffiest powder snow that floats up into the air like tiny bubbles.

Crud: powder snow that is getting heavier by the minute in the sun.

Corduroy: machine-groomed snow that looks like perfect corduroy.

Hero snow: soft, friendly snow, usually corduroy that makes any skier feel like they could win an Olympic medal.

Hardpack: older snow that is firmly packed by the wind, melting and refreezing, or machines.

Windpack: firm snow formed by wind.

Death cookies: hamburger-sized chunks of frozen snow on a trail are often referred to as death cookies in the East; Westerners tend to call them chicken heads.

Corn: old snow that has thawed and re-frozen so many times it becomes rounded pellets. It can be good for skiing.

Frozen granular: a hard surface of old snow that has melted and refrozen into rough chunks and sharp blobs.

Mashed potatoes: heavy, wet, snow that smears like mashed potatoes when you turn to stop in it.

Firn: granular, partially consolidated snow that has passed through one summer melt season but is not yet glacial ice.

Elephant snot: dry snow that turns to the consistency of porridge when it warms up. Also called slurpee pack.

Sierra Cement: heavy, wet snow like in California's Sierra Nevada.

Snow Can Be All Wet

In this experiment you can see how much water comes from two different kinds of snow: snow near the ground and snow on top.

1 Take the two containers outside. Gently scoop snow off the surface of a snow bank to fill one container (try hard not to press down, or squeeze the snow you are scooping). Put on the lid. Mark the container number one.

2 Now dig as far down as you can and scoop snow out of the hole to fill another container. Try hard not to press down, or compress, the snow you are scooping. You want to fill the containers with snow without changing it. Mark the container number two.

3 Bring the containers inside and let the snow melt. When the snow has turned to water, take off the lids. Measure the amount of water in the first container. Write down in your science journal how much water container number one held. Do the same for the water in container number two.

Things to Notice

❊ Did both containers have the same amount of water? Or did one container have more than the other container?

❊ Which container held more water?

❊ What else did you notice about this experiment?

Supplies

two containers of the same size with lids

snow

marker

measuring cups

science journal

Snow is Cold—But Can Keep You Warm!

Did you know that snow can keep you warm? We've already learned that since snowflakes are crystals, they have lots of pointy edges. And when snowflakes land on the ground, the pointy edges of the snowflakes trap a lot of air between them. Just like feathers or fur trap air against an animal's skin and help keep it warm, snow traps the air near the ground. This keeps the ground warmer than the unprotected air above the snow. Many small animals live in burrows and tunnels underneath the snow because it is much warmer than living above the snow.

People also use snow to keep warm. In far northern Canada, the **Inuit** people make houses made of snow, called **igloos**, during hunting trips. They cut blocks of hard snow and place them on top of each other in the shape of a dome to build a solid shelter. Then they add a low tunnel entrance so the wind doesn't blow into it. The heat from the hunters' bodies warms up the inside of the igloo so they stay nice and warm, even if it is really, really cold outside.

Just for laughs

Q: What do you get when you cross a snowman and a shark?

A: Frost bite!

People who like to camp outside in winter sometimes make cozy shelters out of snow called **quinzees**. First the camper makes a huge snow pile, then lets the snow rest for an hour or so. The snow on top of the pile pushes down on snow underneath and pushes out the air. It makes the snow more dense and stronger. Then the camper digs a hole in the side of the snow pile, and hollows out a cozy cave. A quinzee is a good way to stay safe if you are lost in the snow or caught in a storm without shelter.

Words 2 Know

Inuit: native people who live in far northern Canada and Alaska.

igloo: a round home made of blocks of snow.

quinzee: a cavelike shelter made of snow.

Snow Is Delicious!

You can eat snow, if it is clean that is! When snowflakes are falling you can catch them on your tongue. You can have a sugar-on-snow party. It is a tradition in Vermont to have sugar-on-snow during sugaring season. This is when people boil sap from maple trees to make maple syrup and maple sugar. Sugaring season is in late winter and early spring, when snow is usually still on the ground. To celebrate the start of sugaring, go outside and scoop up fresh, clean snow in bowls. Pour maple syrup over the snow and eat it. If you live in a place where it doesn't snow, you can crush ice in a blender to make pretend snow.

Snow is Toasty

Do this experiment to see how well snow keeps the ground warm.

1 Take one of the thermometers and hold it on top of the snow. Write down the temperature in your science journal.

2 Take the other thermometer and put it about three or four inches under the snow. Write down the temperature.

3 Now put the second thermometer underneath the snow as close to the ground as possible. Record the temperature.

Things to notice

❄ Was the temperature on top of the snow higher or lower than the temperature underneath the snow?

❄ Where did you find the highest temperature?

❄ Where did you find the lowest temperature?

❄ What else did you notice about this experiment?

Supplies
2 thermometers
science journal
lots of snow

Winter Weather

Blizzards or breezes? Snowshoes or sandals? What's the winter weather like where you live? It depends on how far you live from the equator.

The closer to the equator you live, the warmer and more mild your winter. The farther north or south you live from the equator, the colder and stormier your winter will be. The harshness of winter might change from year to year. You might have some winters that are colder or warmer than others.

WOW! The place in the world with the most extreme range in temperature during a year is in northeast Siberia. Temperatures there go from minus 90 degrees Fahrenheit (minus 68 degrees Celsius) in the winter to plus 98 degrees Fahrenheit (37 degrees Celsius) in the summer.

What Is Winter Like in North America?

❄ If you live in the Northeast, on the Atlantic Coast, your winter might include a big snowstorm called a northeaster, nicknamed a Nor'Easter. These are big snowstorms. They happen because warm air from the south pushes up over the Atlantic Ocean. The air pulls lots of ocean moisture with it. It hits the cold air of the north and dumps lots of snow, wind, and sometimes rain.

❄ If you live more to the south, you won't see many freezing temperatures. But sometimes cold air moves in from the north and meets the warm air from the Gulf of Mexico. Then you might get freezing temperatures and even a quick snowfall.

❄ If you live in the central part of North America, your winters can be very cold and full of snow. Cold air flows in from the north. It meets the warm air moving from the south. Since there aren't mountains to stop either the warm or cold air, they meet and cause lots of snowstorms.

❄ If you live in the northwestern part of North America, you could get some bad snowstorms. That's because cold air comes off the Rocky Mountains and combines with warm air from the Pacific Ocean. The result can be quick, heavy snowstorms. Usually the closer you live to the ocean, the less snow you get. That's because the air nearer the ocean is warmer and blocks the colder air coming from the north.

❄ If you live in the far north, you will be cold! You will also get lots of snow. Any moisture that comes from the northern oceans meets cold, Arctic air. It turns into snow.

❄ If you live in the far south, you won't notice much of a difference in temperature. Instead, you'll probably be having a dry season, with less rainfall than at other times of the year.

What is Weather?

Weather is not something that happens just when clouds arrive, or when the wind blows, or when it rains or snows. The weather is what the air around the earth is doing all the time. What causes winter weather? Blame it on the sun. Remember that the sun hits the earth at an angle during the winter months.

When the Northern Hemisphere is tilted away from the sun, that means shorter days and cooler temperatures. Those cooler temperatures do more than make you need to wear a coat or mittens. They also affect the weather.

Just for laughs

Q: What did one thermometer say to the other thermometer?

A: You make my temperature rise.

All the air around the planet is warmed by the sun. Remember that the air on earth is constantly moving around. It rises when it becomes warm. It sinks when it gets cold.

Storms happen when lots of cold air meets lots of warm, damp air. The two kinds of air meet and move around each other. This is called **convection**. Convection makes clouds grow. As the clouds grow, they tumble together, and rise and collect with moisture. When the clouds get too heavy, gravity pulls the moisture down to the ground.

Dark clouds are usually storm clouds. Most clouds look white because they reflect the light of the sun. Dark clouds are dark because they are full of water droplets or ice crystals. If there is enough water or ice in a cloud, light can't shine through the cloud, which is why the cloud looks dark. Dark clouds mean that a storm is brewing.

This happens all year round, every day of the week. But why do many places have snow in the winter instead of rain? Because in the winter, the air cools down. Colder air makes the land and oceans colder, too. When the temperature of the air is cold enough the moisture in the clouds freezes. It turns into ice crystals. More moisture attaches to the ice crystals. They grow heavy enough to fall down towards the ground. Sometimes the ice crystal will melt just a bit if it falls through a layer of air that's a bit warmer. This melting acts a little bit like glue. Other ice crystals attach to it on their way down to the ground. That's what makes fluffy snowflakes. At other times, the ice crystals melt too much and then refreeze just as they hit the ground. This is called sleet. Sleet looks like little ice pellets, because that's exactly what it is!

WOW!
The higher the clouds, the better the weather. Clouds are formed by moisture that condenses out of rising air. The higher the air must rise before condensation begins, the drier it is to begin with.

Air Pressure Predicts the Weather

Air pressure is a way that meteorologists can predict what the weather will be. High pressure usually means clear weather. Low pressure usually means stormy weather.

Why? You just learned that warm air rises and cold air sinks. Warm air is less dense, or under less pressure, than cold air. This is why a hot air balloon can rise up into the sky. Hot air is lighter than cool air. As warm air rises, it mixes with cooler air and collects with moisture. Cooler air can't hold as much moisture as warm air can. Rising air reaches a point where it becomes too cool to hold the moisture. The moisture condenses as clouds. If there is enough moisture in the clouds, it will turn to rain—or snow, depending on the temperature. So when the air pressure goes down, it means that warm air is rising. Rising warm air mixing with cold air high up means clouds. And storms.

Winter is a Dry Season Down South

For people who live in the far south, winter doesn't usually mean cold weather or snow. Winter usually means dry weather. From about November to about April, the weather in places just north of the equator is usually dry and sunny. For locations just south of the equator, those same months are rainy.

Why? Because of something called the **Inter-Tropical Convergence Zone** (ITCZ—called "itch."). Winds blowing from the Northern Hemisphere and Southern Hemisphere meet in the tropics. They cause a line of clouds hundreds of miles wide. This band of clouds follows the sun. It moves north in the Northern Hemisphere's summer, and south in the Northern Hemisphere's winter. So during the winter in the northern tropics, the line of clouds is farther south and that makes the weather warm and dry.

Make a Barometer to Predict the Weather

A barometer is a scientific instrument that can help predict the weather by measuring air pressure. This activity will show you how to make a simple barometer.

1 Blow up the balloon and then let the air out. This stretches the balloon so it will easily fit over the mouth of the jar. Cut the balloon in two pieces, just above where it starts to get narrow. Throw away the narrow part.

2 Stretch the balloon over the mouth of the jar. Hold it in place with a rubber band over the balloon around the mouth of the jar. Make sure there are no gaps between the balloon and the jar. You want the jar to be airtight.

3 Tape the straw onto the balloon lid. One end of the straw should be almost all the way across the top of the lid, but not touching the far side. The other end of the straw should stick out past the jar. The tape should be about an inch or so from the end of the straw so it can move.

4 You've just made a barometer! Let's test your barometer and see how it works. Put the barometer on a table or shelf right next to a wall. Tape a piece of paper on the wall next to the jar.

5 Make a mark with your pencil on the piece of paper where the straw is pointing. Write the date next to the mark. Write the date in your science journal and make observations about the weather. Make sure the paper is positioned so there is room above and below the straw. That way you can make more marks.

6 Check your straw each day at the same time, and mark the straw's position on the piece of paper with a different colored pencil each time. Put the date next to the mark.

7 In your science journal, use the same colored pencil to write the date and what the weather is like when you make the mark (for example, "windy," "rainy," "sunny") After a few days, compare the markings and the weather statements you have recorded.

Here's what is happening: When you fit the balloon over the glass to make your barometer, you captured air under a certain pressure. The balloon will show changes in the pressure of the air around you. Higher air pressure pushes the balloon into the jar and makes the straw go up. Lower air pressure will make the air in the jar expand and will bulge the balloon, moving the straw down.

Things to notice

❋ When the straw moved up, what was the weather note you made?

❋ When the straw moved down, what was the weather note you made?

❋ Did you try this experiment during a whole week of dry or stormy weather?

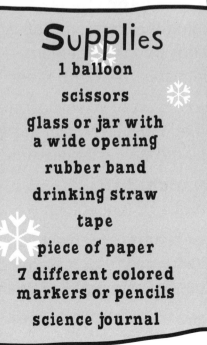

Supplies
1 balloon

scissors

glass or jar with a wide opening

rubber band

drinking straw

tape

piece of paper

7 different colored markers or pencils

science journal

Brr! Winter Wind is Chilly!

You know that winter wind is much colder than summer wind. It makes sense that if the air is colder to begin with, then the wind will be cold, too. But why does a windy winter day feel so much colder than a day at the same temperature without wind? Because of something called the **windchill effect**. When wind blows around you, it pulls away the warm air trapped around your body. That chills you. The faster the wind blows, the faster you lose body heat. Even if the sun is shining, a windy winter day can make you feel very cold, very fast.

If you play outside for a long time in winter, you might get something called frostbite. Frostbite is when skin freezes from being out in the cold for too long. Places on the body that get frostbite most often are noses, ears, cheeks, and fingers. When skin gets nipped by frost, it turns white or yellow and can feel tingly or numb. It is important to warm up your skin if it gets frostbite so it isn't permanently hurt. When you are playing outside, wear several layers and come inside pretty often to warm up. Have a grownup check your fingers and face to make sure they are not getting nipped.

Words 2 Know

convection: when cold air meets warm air and forms clouds.

Inter-Tropical Convergence Zone: the area where the Northern Hemisphere's winds and the Southern Hemisphere's winds meet.

barometer: scientific instrument that can help predict the weather by measuring air pressure.

windchill effect: how the wind makes it feel colder.

anemometer: scientific instrument that meteorologists use to measure wind speed.

Make an Anemometer

Anemometers are scientific instruments that meteorologists use to measure wind speed. In this project you will make a simple anemometer. This anemometer will give you an estimate of how fast the wind is blowing.

Supplies

five 3-ounce paper cups

pen for poking holes

two straight plastic straws

colored marker

small stapler

straight pin

sharp pencil with an eraser

large piece of modeling clay

a watch that shows seconds

1 Take one of the paper cups and poke four equally spaced holes about a quarter inch below the rim. Then punch a hole in the center of the bottom of the cup.

2 Poke one of the straws through two opposite holes in the cup. Then poke the other straw through the other two holes. The two straws will look like an "X" with the cup in the middle.

3 Take one of the other paper cups and color the outside with a marker. You'll use this cup to mark each time the wind turns your anemometer. Now put this cup back with the other cups.

4 Poke one hole in each of these four cups about a half inch below the rim.

5 Take one of the cups and push one end of one of the straws through the hole. The open end of the cup should face either left or right—not up or down. Fold the end of the straw, then staple it to the side of the cup across from the hole. That will help make sure the cup doesn't blow off the straw in the wind.

6 Do this three more times with each of the other cups. Make sure that the open ends of the four cups all face the same direction (either clockwise or counterclockwise) around the center cup.

7 Push the eraser end of the pencil up through the bottom hole in the center cup until it hits the straws. Push the straight pin down through the two straws where they intersect in the middle of the center cup. Push the pin into the end of the pencil eraser as far as it will go. Make sure the straws can spin around on the pencil eraser.

WOW!

The highest wind gust ever recorded was 231 miles per hour (372 kilometers per hour) on top of Mount Washington. This is New Hampshire's tallest mountain.

8 Take your anemometer outside and stick the modeling clay on a surface outside, such as a porch railing, wooden fence rail, a wall, or a rock. Stick the sharpened end of the pencil into the clay so it stands up straight. It is a good idea to make a mark somewhere on the surface so you can tell when your colored cup has made one full spin around.

9 Your anemometer is now ready to go! You won't be able to tell exactly what the wind speed is in miles or kilometers per hour, but you can count how fast your anemometer turns. This will give you a measure of how fast the wind is blowing. Use your watch to count the number of times the colored cup spins around in one minute. That is called revolutions per minute. The kind of anemometers that meteorologists use also count revolutions per minute, then they convert the revolutions per minute into kilometers per hour.

Things to Notice

❄ Is the wind speed different at different times of the day?

❄ If you move your anemometer to a different place, is it windier?

❄ What places seem windier than others?

❄ Do trees or buildings make it more or less windy?

Just for laughs

Q: Why don't mountains get cold in the winter?

A: They wear snow caps.

10 Keep a record of the wind speeds you're measuring for the next few days, and measure the wind speed at different times of the day. You can also measure the wind in different places.

adapt: to make changes or to cope with your environment.

altitude: how high something is, usually measured above sea level.

amphibians: cold-blooded animals like frogs that live on land but breed in the water.

anemometer: scientific instrument used to measure wind speed.

barometer: scientific instrument that helps predict weather by measuring air pressure.

biome: a large area of the earth with a similar climate.

brumate: reptile hibernation.

camouflage: to hide by changing the way you look.

Celsius: a scale of measuring temperature.

climatologist: a scientist who studies and predicts general weather and climate over a long period of time and a large area.

cold-blooded: animals that need warm air or water to keep warm, like frogs and snakes.

condensation: when water cools and condenses into clouds of liquid droplets.

condense: to move from the gas state to the liquid state of water.

coniferous trees: trees that have needle-like leaves and produce cones.

convection: when cold air meets warm air and forms clouds.

deciduous trees: trees that have broad leaves that die and fall off in the fall.

dense: packed tightly.

density: the mass of something compared to how much space it takes up.

desert: the hottest biome that gets very little rain.

diapause: a period of time when insects stop growing or changing.

dormant: to be in a resting and inactive state.

equator: the imaginary line running around the middle of the earth that divides it in two halves, the Northern Hemisphere and the Southern Hemisphere.

evaporate: to change from the liquid state to the gas or vapor state of water.

evergreen trees: trees that keep their leaves all year. Most evergreens are conifers.

expand: to increase in size or to take up more space.

experiment: testing an idea or hypothesis.

Fahrenheit: a scale for measuring temperature.

fall equinox: the official first day of fall, when there is 12 hours of daylight and 12 hours of darkness everywhere.

frostbite: when skin freezes.

grassland: a biome in the temperate zone, covered in tall grass.

hexagon: six-sided shape.

hibernate: to go into a deep sleep for many months with a low body temperature and heart rate.

hypothesis: an unproven idea that tries to explain certain facts or observations.

ice: the solid state of water.

igloo: a round home made of blocks of snow.

Inter-Tropical Convergence Zone: the area where the Northern Hemisphere's winds and the Southern Hemisphere's winds meet.

Inuit: native people who live in far northern Canada or Alaska.

larvae: the wormlike stage of an insect's life.

latitude: how far north or south a location is from the equator. Portland, Oregon, is at 45 degrees latitude north, halfway between the equator and the North Pole.

mammal: a warm-blooded animal covered with hair that is nourished by milk when it's born. Humans, deer, and dogs are all mammals.

meteorologist: a scientist who studies weather patterns and makes weather predictions.

migrate: to travel to the same place at the same time each year

molecule: the tiniest particles that make up objects.

Northern Hemisphere: the half of the earth north of equator.

polar regions: the latitudes around the North Pole and the South Pole.

precipitation: condensed water vapor that falls to the earth's surface in the form of rain, snow, sleet, or hail.

predator: an animal that eats other animals by hunting them.

prey: animals that get eaten by predators.

pupae: the cocoon stage of an insect's life when it changes from one form to another.

quinzee: a cavelike shelter made of snow.

reptile: a cold-blooded animal that crawls on its belly or on short legs like a snake or a lizard.

saturation: when the water falling on land collects in rivers and lakes, soil and porous layers of rock, and much of it flows back into the ocean.

scientific process: the way scientists ask questions and do experiments to try to prove their ideas.

sleet: ice crystals that melt while they fall and then refreeze into ice pellets closer to the ground.

solution: one substance dissolved into another.

Southern Hemisphere: the half of the earth south of equator.

spring equinox: the official first day of spring, when there is 12 hours of daylight and 12 hours of darkness everywhere.

summer solstice: the official first day of summer, when a hemisphere tilts toward the sun as much as it will go. The summer solstice is the longest day of the year.

symmetrical: the same on all sides.

taiga: a biome in the northern part of the temperate zone, with a cold winter and lots of snow.

temperate zone: the latitudes in between the tropics and the polar regions.

temperate forest: a biome with a hot summer, cool spring and fall, and a cold winter.

torpor: a state of inactivity like a deep sleep.

tropical rainforest: a biome where it is warm all the time.

tropics: near the equator.

tundra: the coldest biome, around the North Pole.

vibrate: to move back and forth very, very quickly.

warm-blooded: animals that can keep themselves warm with their own body heat, like birds and bears.

water cycle: the continuous movement of water from the earth to the clouds and back to earth again.

water vapor: the gas state of water.

windchill effect: how the wind makes it feel colder.

winter: the season between fall and spring, from about December 21 to March 21 in the Northern Hemisphere and from about June 21 to September 21 in the Southern Hemisphere.

winter solstice: the official first day of winter when a hemisphere tilts as far away from the sun as it will go. The winter solstice is the shortest day of the year.

Books

Branley, Franklyn M. *Air Is All Around You.* New York: Thomas Y. Crowell, 1962.

Branley, Franklyn M. *Down Comes The Rain.* New York: Harper Collins Publishers, 1963.

Dorros, Arthur. *Feel the Wind.* New York: Thomas Y. Crowell, 1989.

Drake, Jane and Ann Love. *Snow Amazing: Cool Facts and Warm Tales.* Canada: Tundra Books, 2004.

Elsom, Derek. *Weather Explained: A Beginner's Guide to the Elements.* New York: Henry Hold and Company, 1997.

Lerner, Carol. *A Forest Year.* New York: William Morrow and Company Inc., 1987.

McMillan, Bruce. *The Weather Sky.* New York: Farrar Straus Giroux, 1991.

McVey, Vicki. *The Sierra Club Book of Weatherwisdom.* San Francisco: Sierra Club Books and Boston, Toronto, London: Little, Brown and Co., 1991.

Pope, Joyce and Dr. Philip Whitfield. *Why Do The Seasons Change?: Questions on Nature's Rhythms and Cycles answered by the Natural History Museum.* New York: Viking Penguin Inc., 1987.

Shedd, Warner. *The Kids Wildlife Book.* Vermont: Williamson Publishing, 1994.

Simon, Seymour. *Weather.* New York: Morrow Junior Books, 1993.

Vogel, Carole G. *Nature's Fury: Eyewitness Reports of Natural Disasters.* Scholastic Inc., 2000.

Web Sites

The Weather Channel
http://www.weatherclassroom.com

Weather Wiz Kids
http://www.weatherwizkids.com

National Geographic Kids
http://kids.nationalgeographic.com

The Audubon Society
http://www.audubon.org/educate

The Museum of Science, Boston
http://www.mos.org

The Exploratorium
http://www.exploratorium.edu

USDA Forest Service
http://www.fs.fed.us

Scholastic
http://www.scholastic.com/kids/weather

Wikipedia
http://www.wikipedia.org

World Book Encyclopedia
http://www.worldbook.com/features/seasons/html/seasons.htm

The Library of Congress
http://www.loc.gov

The Academy of Natural Sciences
http://www.ansp.org

The Carnegie Science Museum
http://www.carnegiesciencecenter.org

The University of Richmond
http://oncampus.richmond.edu/academics/education/projects/webunits/biomes/biomes.html

Missouri Botanical Garden
http://www.mbgnet.net/